THE POWER OF APPRECIATIVE COMMUNICATION

A GUIDE FOR SELF-REFLECTION AND FACILITATION

ARPI ARUS

Published by Garnan Guchaque

Fairfield, Vermont, USA

Copyright © 2025 Arpi Arus & Garnan Guchaque

Artist: Milena Avetisyan

All rights reserved. No part of this book may be reproduced, distributed, or transmitted in any form or by any means, including photocopying, recording, or other electronic or mechanical methods, without the prior written permission of the publisher, except in the case of brief quotations embodied in critical reviews and certain other noncommercial uses permitted by copyright law.

English version

For feedback or inquiries, contact: arpi.arus.edu@gmail.com
garnanguchaque@gmail.com

The views and opinions expressed in this book are those of the author and do not necessarily reflect the official policy of Garnan Guchaque.

CONTENTS

Acknowledgments   ix
Synopsis   xi
Introduction   xiii

PART I
POSITIVE COMMUNICATION

LESSON 1: COMMUNICATION STYLES	3
Assertive	4
Aggressive	4
Passive	4
Passive–Aggressive	5
Exercise 1.1 — Communication Styles	5
Examples of Assertive Dialogue:	6
LESSON 2: THE SECRETS OF ASSERTIVE COMMUNICATION	8
Difference between Assertive and Aggressive Styles	8
Difference Between Assertive and Passive–Aggressive Styles	10
Exercise 2.1 — Practicing Assertive Communication	11
LESSON 3: THE POWER OF ASKING INSTEAD OF ASSUMING	12
Comfort or a Solution?	13
Do you need help?	15
LESSON 4: STRATEGIC QUESTIONING	17
About the question "Why?"	18
Exercise 4.1 — Practicing Strategic Questioning	19

LESSON 5: WITHHOLD YOUR INITIAL REACTION	21
How our brains work	21
Culpability	22
Intent to Harm	24
Exercise 5.1 — The Drop of Honey (adapted from Hovahnnes Toumanyan's poem)	26
LESSON 6: ASSUME GOOD INTENT	30
Exercise 6.1 — Withhold Your Reaction	32
Exercise 6.2 — The Meeting of Mice (adapted from Atabek Khnkoyan's poem)	32
LESSON 7: VERIFY YOUR ASSUMPTION	34
A Half-Cup of Water	35

PART II
THE POWER OF APPRECIATION

LESSON 8: THE PRINCIPLES OF APPRECIATIVE INQUIRY	39
Exercise 8.1 — Find a positive topic	42
LESSON 9: CONSTRUCTIONIST PRINCIPLE	44
Giving Constructive Feedback	45
Stalinism	48
Exercise 9.1 — Start with "Yes"	51
Exercise 9.2 — Ability to Reframe	52
LESSON 10: SIMULTANEITY PRINCIPLE	53
Reframing the Problem	53
Exercise 10.1 — Reframe and Elevate	54
How to make the reframed topic more exciting?	55
Changing Object with Subject	57
Exercise 10.2 — Elevate the Topic	59
James F. Finckenauer's Theory of Legal Socialization.	59

LESSON 11: POETIC PRINCIPLE	62
Is the lack of bad news considered good news?	64
Does the Expression "Fake it till you make it" work?	65
Exercise 11.1 — Find Something Nice	67
LESSON 12: ANTICIPATORY PRINCIPLE	68
Suggested Norms to Encourage Participation	72
LESSON 13: POSITIVITY PRINCIPLE	74
Exercise 13.1 — Jacqueline Kelm's "Exercise of Joy" Practice	78
LESSON 14: THE MAGIC FORMULA FOR EMPOWERING QUESTIONS	79
Exercise 14.1 — Practicing Appreciative Questioning	82
Questions for Managing Up	83
Conclusion	85
Appendix A: Selected Exercise Answers	91
Appendix B: Bibliography	97
About the Author	99
About the Artist	101

ACKNOWLEDGMENTS

This book is dedicated to the group of smart, considerate, inquisitive, mischievous, funny, and endlessly resilient children of Artsakh who helped me to shape and structure it.

In September of 2022, we started our regular online classes in Appreciative Inquiry with the middle- and high-school children from various villages in the Martuni and Martakert districts of Artsakh, also known as Nagorno Karabakh. I used Jacqueline Kelm's book, *The Joy of Appreciative Living: Your 28-Day Plan to Greater Happiness Using the Principles of Appreciative Inquiry* (1) and created a ten-slide presentation with the intention of discussing one slide a week over the course of 10 weeks. The information from those slides is presented at the beginning of each Lesson in Part 2 of this book. (I called them "Jacqueline Kelm's Commandments.")

On December 12, 2022, Artsakh was cut from the rest of the world and the children of Artsakh became hostages of dirty politics that took the lives of their parents and relatives. We were about to finish the class and go to the Holiday Season celebrations when the blockade of the Lachin Corridor started. The students asked me to continue our weekly classes throughout the Christmas vacation. The structure of the classes that followed was based on their questions and, especially, their needs at that traumatic time.

I am immensely thankful to my students and their local

teachers who gave me lessons in resilience, forgiveness, and deep, sincere appreciation.

I am also infinitely thankful to the Armenian communities in Vermont, Massachusetts and California, as well as to US legislators, the UN, and the Red Cross for helping to keep these children alive during their forcible displacement from their home.

A separate acknowledgment should be given to Doctor Lucia Babayants, who provided huge psychological support and grief therapy once the children arrived safely in Armenia.

Finally, my deepest thankfulness goes to the people of Armenia, who hosted my students and their parents, and opened their hearts for them to make sure their relocation and transition took place as smoothly and painlessly as possible.

SYNOPSIS

This 14-lesson book equips educators and facilitators with the tools to teach Appreciative Inquiry in diverse multicultural settings. Designed as a practical guide, it offers 15 engaging exercises to cultivate a positive mindset and develop a valuable skill, empowering others through inspirational, thought-provoking questions. By fostering strengths-based conversations, this book helps trainers create inclusive learning environments where participants can explore possibilities, build connections, and drive meaningful change. Whether working with students, community groups, or professional teams, this resource provides a structured yet adaptable approach to facilitating transformative dialogue. The first part of the book offers tools that help you to work on yourself and understand better the essence of your interaction with others. The second part of the book builds on that skill and offers additional tools to help others to see their strengths, get inspired, and enter into a transformative dialogue with you.

INTRODUCTION

Who would benefit from this book?

This book is beneficial for the educators and facilitators of Appreciative Inquiry working with a mixed group of students with diverse cultural backgrounds - whether a specific generation of trainees or participants from different cultural backgrounds. Many activities included in this book stem from my experiences learning lessons on Intercultural Communication at the School for International Training (Brattleboro, VT) as well as training programs developed by the United Nations, various non-governmental organizations, and the Vermont Refugee Resettlement Program. This book also includes some exercises offered in the Appreciative Inquiry Practitioner's Certification course by The David Cooperrider Center of Appreciative Inquiry.

Introduction

How is this book different from other strengths-based facilitation guides?

This book is uniquely designed to reflect the real-life challenges faced by individuals in war-affected areas when introduced to traditional Appreciative Inquiry. In such environments, where adversity and hardship dominate daily life, the concept of focusing on strengths and opportunities can feel unfamiliar—even unattainable.

Through experience, it becomes clear that before individuals can embrace a strengths-based approach, they often need space to express their struggles. This book acknowledges that reality. Part One is specifically designed to help facilitators guide participants through acknowledging and processing negative experiences, creating a bridge toward solution-focused thinking and positive transformation.

How to use this book

Begin with daily appreciation exercises suggested by Jackueline Kelm. The details are listed in Exercise 13.1. Start on day one and continue doing it daily throughout the course.

This book consists of two parts.

Part 1 of this book focuses on self-reflection, offering exercises to build a positive mindset. It helps develop control over one's reactions and responses to others.

Part 2 of this book explores actions that influence others' reactions. Having learned how to respond positively in Part 1, this section helps develop skills to inspire positive responses from others.

During classroom training, we built our skills collaboratively —analyzing and solving real problems as a group. A common exercise involves writing problems on paper, placing them in a hat, and drawing one at a time for discussion. Practicing with various problems, looking at things from different angles, exploring each other's perspectives helps tremendously to build the necessary skill set. A digital alternative to this exercise can use shared Google documents, or message platforms. If practicing alone, artificial intelligence can generate additional exercises featuring unexpected topics.

Some exercises include suggested answers in Appendix A. These answers are merely suggestions. We encourage you to work through the exercises on your own first—you may discover better solutions than those provided in the appendix.

How to use the references

For the references, we have used a numbered reference list following the Vancouver system. Each source is listed in the Bibliography (Appendix B) with a corresponding number, which serves as its reference location. In the parentheses following certain sentences in the book, the first number indicates the source's position in the Bibliography, while the second number represents the specific page or page range where the relevant information can be found.

What is Positive Psychology?

Positive psychology is a branch of psychology that focuses on the study and promotion of positive emotions, strengths, and virtues. It emphasizes the importance of understanding and cultivating human strengths and virtues to enhance overall well-being and happiness.

Introduction

Martin Seligman, the founding father of positive psychology, credited Mihaly Csikszentmihaly as "the brains behind it." (2,37)

Key areas within positive psychology include resilience, optimism, gratitude, mindfulness, compassion, and the pursuit of personal strengths and virtues. Researchers and practitioners in this field seek to uncover ways to foster positive emotions, build fulfilling relationships, and facilitate personal growth.

The goal of Positive Psychology is to enhance individuals' quality of life and contribute to the creation of a flourishing society.

What is Appreciative Inquiry?

Appreciative Inquiry is an approach rooted in Positive Psychology, designed specifically for organizational development. It focuses on crafting powerful questions that highlight strengths and possibilities rather than problems. By shifting the focus from a defensive stance to a solution-based perspective, Appreciative Inquiry fosters constructive change.

For example, in a half-cup of water situation, the Appreciative Inquiry practitioner would not ask, "What do you see?" Rather, she would ask, "What are the best qualities of the water that you see in that cup?"

The concept of Appreciative Inquiry was developed by David Cooperrider and Suresh Srivastva in the 1980s. (3, xxvii) It originated from a realization that the questions we ask shape the answer we receive and therefore significantly influence the information, ideas and results that emerge. Appreciative Inquiry encourages asking positive, constructive questions to envision and create a positive future for an organization or community.

While Positive Psychology focuses on the importance of

Introduction

concentrating on positive aspects in human development, Appreciative Inquiry applies these principles to organizational change and development.

PART I
POSITIVE COMMUNICATION

LESSON 1: COMMUNICATION STYLES

I was first exposed to this lesson at the Vermont Refugee Resettlement Program during an immigrant community integration training session. The US education system tries to incorporate awareness of various communication styles as early as kindergarten or daycare. However, since this is a relatively recent development, older generations may be less familiar with these styles of communication. In today's multicultural corporate world, where employees come from diverse cultural backgrounds and multiple generations work together, this lesson is often included as part of orientation training.

Styles of communication explored in these sessions often include:

- Assertive
- Aggressive
- Passive
- Passive–aggressive

Assertive

The assertive style of communication is expressing your thoughts and feelings in a clear, confident, and respectful manner, while also acknowledging the thoughts and feelings of others. An assertive person stands up for their own rights without violating the rights of others.

Example: "I understand that we have different opinions, but I believe my idea could also be beneficial for the project. Can we discuss it further?"

Aggressive

The aggressive style of communication is one in which thoughts and feelings are expressed in a forceful, disrespectful, and often hostile manner, without considering the feelings or rights of others. It can involve dominating, intimidating, or humiliating others.

Example: "My idea is the only one that matters. We're doing it my way, and that's final!"

Passive

The passive style of communication avoids conflict and is characterized by being unwilling to express thoughts and feelings directly. A passive person often puts others' needs before their own and may struggle to communicate their own desires.

Example: "I don't mind, we can do whatever you want for our project."

Passive–Aggressive

This style involves indirectly expressing negative feelings or resentment through actions and subtle, unassertive behavior. It can include sarcasm, procrastination, or subtle sabotage.

Example: "Oh, don't worry about me. I'm used to doing all the work by myself anyway."

Exercise 1.1 — Communication Styles

Determine the communication style. Change passive, aggressive, and passive–aggressive responses into assertive communication.

1. Student: "Can I borrow your pencil?"
   Response: "Fine, take it. Not like I need it anyway."

2. Student: "I don't agree with the group's decision."
   Response: "I respect your opinion, and I think it's important to discuss different perspectives."

3. Student: "You never listen to me!"
   Response: "I'm sorry if it seems that way. Let's talk about how we can communicate better."

4. Student: "I think we should do it my way."
   Response: "I appreciate your input. Let's find a compromise that works for everyone."

5. Student: "I won't do it! I hate these stupid group projects!"
   Response: "It's okay, I'll just do it myself as usual."

6. Student: "I want to join the game."
   Response: "Sorry, I got here first. Find another one."

7. Student: "I don't like when you interrupt me."
   Response: "Well, if you talked faster, maybe I wouldn't have to."

8. Student: "I'm disappointed that you didn't help with the assignment."
   Response: "Oh, I didn't know you needed help. You should've told me."

9. Student: "I insist on handling this part of the project."
   Response: "You always take over everything! Fine, do it your way."

10. Student: "I made a mistake, and I'll correct it."
    Response: "Who cares? What's the big deal?"

Examples of Assertive Dialogue:

1. "I want to handle this part of the project."
   Response: "I appreciate your willingness, but I believe I am best suited to handle this part. However, I'm open to collaborating on other aspects."

2. "I think we should reschedule the meeting."
   Response: "I understand your point, but I believe sticking to

the original schedule is crucial. Let's find a way to address everyone's concerns without delaying the progress."

3. "You never consider my suggestions."
Response: "I value your input, and I believe we can find a way to incorporate your suggestions along with the team's overall goals."

4. "I don't like how you talk to me in front of others."
Response: "I'd prefer to discuss our interactions in a private setting. It's essential to me that we maintain a respectful and constructive communication environment."

5. "You should always agree with the majority."
Response: "I respectfully disagree. I believe it's important to express diverse viewpoints, even when they differ from the majority. Let's discuss why diversity of opinion strengthens our decisions."

LESSON 2: THE SECRETS OF ASSERTIVE COMMUNICATION

Difference between Assertive and Aggressive Styles

Assertive and aggressive styles have one thing in common: in both, you make an effort to stand your ground. Making your case and getting your point across is important in both approaches. However, while aggressive is non-compromising, an assertive style invites cooperation in some areas. The goal of the aggressive style is to win the argument and end the conversation. The assertive style is an invitation to continue the discussion.

One of the best ways to get your point across in a non-threatening way is to speak in the first person. Try to express your thoughts using the pronouns "I," "me," and "my" instead of "you," "your," and "yours." First-person pronouns tend to sound less threatening than accusing someone directly by using "you." When you start with "you," it may be perceived as a threat or accusation. This puts the listener on the defensive and the probability of receiving a push back increases.

A statement made in the first person, on the other hand,

offers the listener a point of view from a new angle and is perceived as being more a value rather than a threat.

Listen to the difference between these two statements:

Statement 1: "You never listen to me!"
Statement 2: "I have noticed that my voice cannot be heard in some cases. Can we find a more effective way to understand each other?"

The formula for assertive communication is:

1. Mention the facts (explain what happened rather than what "you" did to me).
2. Note the impact of these facts on you (explain how "I" felt about that fact rather than what "you" did to me).

For example, a child wanting ice cream and seeing that there is none in the freezer can cry and say to their parents: "You never buy me ice cream! You only think about yourself and never take my opinion into account!"

This puts the parents into a defensive position.

A child practicing assertive style of communication may use the formula "stick to the facts and explain their impact on you":

"When I see there is no ice cream in the fridge, my heart breaks into pieces!"

In the second sentence, the absence of ice cream in the refrigerator is an indisputable fact. No one will object to the child saying that there is no ice cream in the freezer, if it really isn't there. Perhaps the conversation will develop in a different way, the reasons for the lack of ice cream may be explained, and there will be an opportunity to negotiate.

The fact that your heart is breaking into pieces will also be hard to argue with. You are not accusing someone else, you are simply describing your situation; you are expressing your feelings to the other person. In this case, instead of arguing with you, the possibility of continuing negotiations with you prevails.

Difference Between Assertive and Passive–Aggressive Styles

In assertive communication, thoughts are expressed honestly and directly. If you really feel that the lack of ice cream broke your heart, or those are the only words you could find at that moment to describe your feelings, then this can be considered assertive communication. However, if this is a ploy to make your parents feel guilty and stop objecting to your requests the next time they pass an ice cream parlor, then your expression becomes passive–aggressive.

From the moment a sincere conversation turns into trickery or manipulation, your demeanor changes from assertive to passive–aggressive. Passive–aggressive expressions may include:

"You will bring me to the door of the grave."
"You are killing me!"
"If you don't talk to me, I will jump off a cliff," and
so on.

The next time you find yourself in an argument, instead of saying, "You're insulting me," try: "I felt offended." This subtle shift in language opens up new perspectives and encourages constructive dialogue. The goal is to foster a more positive and collaborative conversation. You have the power to turn a potentially confrontational monologue into a constructive dialogue.

Lesson 2: The Secrets of Assertive Communication

Exercise 2.1 — Practicing Assertive Communication

How could you change the following statements to make them more constructive and less threatening or offensive?

1. "You always ruin my plans."
2. "You are lazy; you never help me with the housework."
3. "You're always late, and that's disrespectful."
4. "You're such a slacker in the group project!"
5. "You never appreciate what I do for you!"
6. "You make everything about yourself!"
7. "You're always interrupting me!"
8. "You're such a gossip; you talk behind everyone's back!"
9. "You never support me in my decisions!"

(Suggested answers are provided in Appendix A to facilitate discussion and reflection.)

LESSON 3: THE POWER OF ASKING INSTEAD OF ASSUMING

In the previous section we discussed the power of using "I" statements and avoiding "you" statements. In other words, when something needs to be cleared up, it is better to talk about yourself, and what you saw or felt, rather than what you think the other person saw, felt, or did. When making statements, talking in first person is crucial.

However, dialogue between two people requires us to acknowledge that the other person also has feelings and frustrations. So, asking how they are doing, what they feel, and what their plans are comprise very important questions for establishing open channels of communication. These questions are always asked in second person. This means that, instead of assuming what they did or why they did it, it is better to ask them directly.

Consider the classical example of two children fighting over one orange. If their mother assumed they both wanted to eat the orange, she would decide to divide it in half. Why would she make that assumption? Possibly because that is what she would do if she had another orange, or because juicing it would not stretch that much for two children, or maybe because she would rather see her children eat the orange than play soccer with it. But these assumptions are irrelevant to the core question.

Fortunately, in the classic version of this example the mother chose to ask her children why they want the orange instead of making irrelevant assumptions. It turned out that one of the children needed rind to bake orange cookies while the other was thirsty and wanted to juice the orange. Thus, a simple question before making the final decision allowed this mother to take care of both of her children's needs, 100 %.

If their mother had assumed that they both wanted to eat the orange and decided to divide it in half, she would have missed the nuances of their needs. The child who wanted the peel for baking orange cookies would have ended up baking half-flavored cookies, and the one who thirsted for the juice would only have had a fraction of what they needed. By questioning why they wanted the orange, the mother unlocked a more comprehensive understanding of their desires.

Asking allows for a deeper comprehension of the needs, motivations, and goals of others. It helps to avoid misinterpretation and miscommunication. Asking demonstrates a genuine interest in others' perspectives, fostering trust and strengthening relationships. Asking encourages inclusivity by ensuring that all voices are heard. In collaborative settings, asking questions promotes more effective problem-solving. It encourages the exploration of diverse viewpoints and creative solutions.

Comfort or a Solution?

In our quest to support others, we often jump to provide solutions without fully understanding what the person truly needs. Sometimes, what people seek is not a fix to their problem but rather someone to listen, understand, and offer comfort. In this chapter we explore the importance of asking the question: "Do you need comfort or a solution?" before offering advice. Let's begin by acknowledging that sometimes the greatest support we can provide is simply being there for someone.

Consider this dialogue:

- Person A: "I'm feeling overwhelmed with all of my responsibilities."
- Person B: "You need to manage your time better. Have you tried making a schedule?"

What if Person B tried this instead?

- Person B: "Feeling overwhelmed with responsibilities can be tough. Do you want to vent about what's on your plate, or are you open to brainstorming ways to lighten the load?"

Asking whether someone needs comfort or a solution before offering advice can make a significant difference in how our support is received. It shows empathy, respect, and a genuine desire to meet the person's needs effectively.

Why Understanding Needs is Crucial.

1. It validates emotions: this reassures others that it's okay to feel the way they do.
2. It helps build trust: by listening and providing comfort, we strengthen our relationships with others,

and foster an environment where they feel safe to share their struggles.
3. It indicates that we respect their autonomy: asking whether someone wants a solution empowers them to make decisions about their own situation.

Do you need help?

Another very important item to check before offering is: "Do you need help?"

Asking this before offering assistance is crucial for several reasons:

1. Respecting Autonomy: Asking first respects the individual's autonomy and agency. It acknowledges that they are capable of making their own decisions and allows them to express their needs or preferences.
2. Avoiding Assumptions: Without asking, we may assume incorrectly that someone needs help when they don't, or vice versa. By asking first, we avoid making assumptions and ensure that our assistance is actually wanted and helpful.
3. Empowering Others: Asking empowers the person to communicate their needs and preferences. It gives them a sense of control over the situation and fosters a collaborative approach to problem-solving or support.
4. Building Trust: By asking if someone needs help, we demonstrate genuine concern and respect for their boundaries. This builds trust and strengthens the relationship, as the individual feels understood and valued.

5. Communicating Effectively: Asking opens up dialogue and encourages clear communication. It allows both parties to understand each other's perspectives and ensures that any assistance offered is tailored to the specific needs of the other person.

Overall, asking, "Do you need help?" before offering assistance promotes respect, autonomy, trust, and effective communication, ultimately leading to more meaningful and supportive interactions.

LESSON 4: STRATEGIC QUESTIONING

Strategic questioning is a method introduced by Fran Peavey. (4) The method, originally used in therapy groups, was applied by Fran Peavey to team development. The main idea is to help a team member find an answer to a question without giving direct advice. The person searching for solutions explains the issue to the support group and the rest of the group members start asking clarifying questions. The main rule is that the team members cannot give advice; they can only ask questions.

There are two levels of questions that they can ask.

Level One questions are questions to understand the setting. What happened? Who were the main actors? When did this happen? Who else was there? How did this happen? And so on.

Level Two questions are the questions that are used to look for alternative solutions. Have you tried this? What do you think would happen if you tried that? You didn't try this because of reason "A" or reason "B"? Etc.

Any solution that the supporting team member(s) can think of has to be posed in the form of a question. This is the main rule of the game: no advice; only questions. Sometimes the person searching for clarity may find a solution to their problem; sometimes, they don't. But the main point is: once they find it, they own the solution. They are not following somebody's advice; but making a decision that they think is most applicable to their situation.

About the question "Why?"

In strategic questioning, Fran Peavey suggests avoiding the question "why?" The reason is very simple. If you have a team of 5–6 people helping you to find the solution, you may try to learn their opinions from their questions. This learning is not in the form of a solution or advice; the learning comes from the question. In other worlds, the question should probe a solution. The question "why" is not a question that moves you. It does not necessarily help you to shift your mind towards considering an alternative situation.

However, the question "why" is a good clarifying question. It is a helpful level one question when your team members try to understand the situation.

The question why is also very good when you ask it yourself. It helps you to get to the root of the problem. Why do I avoid working with this person? Is it because they are a bad team-player, or because their accent reminds me of my neighbor who screams at me all of the time? Why can't I write this essay? Why don't I like the topic? Why don't I find it engaging? You might need to ask this "why" question of yourself about five times until you get to the root of the problem.

However, you are able to ask this chain of "why" questions of yourself on your own. Once you have a team of supporting members, you want to pick their brains. You have a team of people (project stakeholders) with their own experiences and solutions, often dying to give you advice. Let them ask you questions that reflect their own responses to the situations, using their own experiences and their own solutions. That will help them to release their urge to give you advice. That will pour out for you a wide range of alternative solutions. That will allow you to think of different outcomes. And that will help you find your own solution, and own that solution.

So, the chain of questions that begin with "why" is good when you ask those questions yourself in order to identify the root cause. It is okay as a level-one question when your team members are trying to clarify the situation. Once it comes to level two questions, Fran Peavey suggests avoiding "why" questions.

Exercise 4.1 — Practicing Strategic Questioning

This exercise is taken from Ryland White's class on Intercultural Communication, taught at the School for International Training (Burlington, Vermont, USA.) This exercise is done in a group of 5–6 people.

For each group meeting, have one person seeking clearance, and let the rest of the group ask questions. Start with the words: "I am seeking clearance on the following issue…" Describe your issue. In order to save time on Level One questions, you may supply the team members with a paragraph describing the issue. Let your team mates read your paragraph and start asking questions. The team mates should start with Level One questions to understand the situation. Depending on how well the initial paragraph is written, this may take only a couple of questions. The transition to Level Two questions can be undetectable, without having to label the questions as Level One or Level Two. Some teammates might be unclear about the situation and ask

Level One questions, while others who have experienced something similar in the past could jump directly into *moving* questions. Continue this exercise until you clarify for yourself the answer to your question, or put a time limitation of 45 to 60 minutes. The number of meetings should be equal to the number of team members, so that each gets a chance to experience the storm of questions.

Unlike brainstorming, where you have one question and a storm of answers, this model helps you to find one answer through the storm of questions. If you find a specific line of questions particularly helpful, you may ask your teammates to continue asking questions in that direction. At the end of the session tell them whether there was clearness on your issue or not. Also, tell them specifically which questions helped you to shift your mindset and explore solutions in a specific direction.

LESSON 5: WITHHOLD YOUR INITIAL REACTION

In all previous lessons, we have discussed the importance of asking instead of assuming. However, it is not that easy to ask neutral, objective questions. Often, when something unclear appears in front of us, it puts us into flight-or-fight mode. We get defensive and we may ask offensive questions. It is very important to train our brain to withhold the urge for that initial reaction.

How our brains work

Don't get me wrong, the flight-or-fight reaction is what allowed previous generations to survive. Our ancestors living in caves had to scan for danger before they could allow themselves to enjoy a beautiful sunset. Through natural selection, those who scanned for danger first, survived. They had children who needed to scan for danger first, in order to survive. So it is only natural that you scan for danger as soon as you feel some initial vibes that something isn't clear. We assess threats instinctively. Whenever we are under immediate attack, assessing correctly whether to hide, run away, or stand and fight is what will save our lives.

However, when we are assigned to a team, this instinctual reaction might not be helpful. When working towards a common goal, reacting aggressively can hinder problem-solving and teamwork. In peaceful conditions, it is essential to recognize our initial negative reactions and withhold the urge to respond immediately. This does not mean ignoring feelings, but rather delaying a reaction until it is appropriately assessed.

Remember, you cannot hold someone culpable for your aggressive behaviour just because you were not able to hold off your initial reaction.

Culpability

In the modern world, the legal definition of culpability often depends on whether offenses fall under the same statute. If someone starts a fight with a simple assault and you respond with the same level of force, you may be able to argue that they are culpable for initiating the altercation. However, if they commit a minor assault and you retaliate with aggravated assault, they cannot be held culpable for your excessive response.

Our instinct during a conflict is to respond disproportionately in order to incapacitate the opponent and survive. This textbook does not offer survival tactics for fights; rather, it aims to help prevent conflicts from escalating.

In determining culpability, it is important to consider the following two questions:

1. Did both parties commit an illegal act?
2. If yes, did both actions fall under the same legal statute?

Lesson 5: Withhold Your Initial Reaction

Why is this important? Asking these questions helps avoid blaming victims for being victimized.

For example:

- "It is your fault the perpetrator hit you because you wore the wrong color lipstick!"
    - Wearing any color of lipstick is legal; hitting is illegal.

- "It is your fault my president started a war against yours! Didn't you know my president dislikes your president? Why did you vote for him?"
    - Voting is legal and constitutional; starting a war and committing atrocities are crimes against humanity.

- "It is your fault we started ethnic cleansing against you! Why did representatives of your ethnicity in our country initiate a referendum for independence?"
    - Exercising the right to self-determination within the constitution is legal. Ethnic cleansing, planned and executed by a government, is a crime under international law.

Understanding culpability is crucial in distinguishing perpetrators from victims. Determining responsibility is not always a matter of who initiated an event but who first broke the law. When a chain of illegal acts occurs, it is important to analyze whether they fall within the same legal framework.

Intent to Harm

> "All men are created equal and have the right to life, liberty, and the pursuit of happiness."
>
> — THOMAS JEFFERSON

Consider this situation. A 12 year old boy (let's call him Ayb) wants to say "hello" to his classmate Ben and shake his hand. Ben refuses to shake Ayb's hand. Ayb feels so hurt that he decides to hit Ben in order to punish him.

There are two dimensions to the situation: one is the legal aspect and the other is emotional.

- Legally, there is no justification for what Ayb did. Ben did not want to shake the hand; there is no legal requirement to shake somebody's hand. Maybe he doesn't want to spread germs. Maybe he doesn't trust Ayb; he's afraid that if he stretches his hand, Ayb may hurt his hand, etc. There could be thousands of other reasons why Ben does not want to shake Ayb's hand. He doesn't need to explain or justify why he doesn't want to shake somebody's hand. It is sufficient to say he does not want to, without explanation. After all, Thomas Jefferson said that he has a right to pursue his happiness, so if not shaking someone's hand makes him happy that's what he has a right to do.
- Emotionally, Ayb feels rejected. However, responding with physical assault is illegal and punishable.

Lesson 5: Withhold Your Initial Reaction

Therefore, "Ben hurt my feelings; that is why I hit him," is not a justification.

But what if Ben knew that not shaking Ayb's hand would hurt his feelings? What if he was willingly and knowingly hurting that person's feelings?

Legally, this information is irrelevant. For any law enforcement officer, the task is to determine at what point the law was broken and arrest the person who broke the law.

An educator's task, however, is to make sure that this doesn't happen again and mitigate the problem. This includes making sure that the children don't hurt each other's feelings. Even though it is not a legal requirement, emotional harm can foster passive–aggressive behaviour and future conflicts.

So the educator has two tasks here because there are two parties involved.

First, the educator should explain to Ayb that hitting is wrong and illegal. Ben's refusal did not violate Ayb's rights; Ayb must adjust his attitude towards rejection. Also, the educator needs to explain that Ben's refusal to shake Ayb's hand is not illegal. It is important here to say that Ayb can not change Ben; all he can do is to change his own attitude. The educator might want to explain that if Ayb wants to shake hands with Ben, Ayb should probably think about building trust first.

The educator's second task is addressing Ayb's hurt feelings which resulted from Ben's rejection of his handshake. To avoid the appearance of victim blaming, this should be done without singling out Ben in front of Ayb. However, in a separate conversation with Ben, the educator should make an effort to determine whether Ben's refusal was solely to hurt Ayb. Ben may have valid reasons for not wanting to shake hands, but knowingly, willingly, and intentionally hurting someone's feelings can quickly escalate the situation.

The situation becomes more complex when we examine the intent to harm in legal cases. Crimes involving moral turpitude (intentional harm) differ from unintentional violations.

For example:

1. Driver 1 accidentally hits another car.
2. Driver 2 intentionally crashes into another car.

Let's say both cars were empty and both accidents caused the same amount of property damage.

What is the difference between these two crimes?

While there are higher chances that, after being punished Driver 1 will learn his lesson and try to drive more carefully, it is harder to predict the follow-on actions for Driver 2. Laws are stricter on crimes involving moral turpitude, as perpetrators often show little remorse and a higher likelihood of reoffending. Whenever there is an intention to harm somebody's life, health, or property, the probability to correct the perpetrator becomes lower. Punishment may only make the perpetrator smarter in the next attack.

Similarly, individuals who intentionally hurt others emotionally, even without breaking laws, may need to be reminded of the long-term consequences of their actions.

Exercise 5.1 — The Drop of Honey (adapted from Hovahnnes Toumanyan's poem)

A shepherd from a mountainous village comes to the valley to buy a jar of honey. He comes with his shepherd dog. The store owner has a cat. When the store owner puts the honey in a jar

Lesson 5: Withhold Your Initial Reaction

for the buyer, a drop of honey falls. A fly lands on that drop. The cat jumps on the fly and kills it. The dog jumps on the cat and kills it. The angry store owner kills the shepherd's dog. The dog owner kills the store owner in revenge. The villagers from the valley run to help their compatriot and kill the shepherd. The villagers from the mountainous village run down to the valley to support their shepherd and kill valley villagers. These two villages belong to two different kingdoms. When the king of the valley villagers hears that the mountainous people attacked his village, he sends an army to attack mountainous people. Then the king from the mountainous country sends an army to attack the valley people. A century-long war lasts between these two kingdoms. They fight and hate each other for several generations. Both kingdoms disappear. Centuries later, historians wonder what started the war.

Question 1:

Consider each crime separately and answer the following questions:

1. Did both parties commit illegal acts?
2. If yes, do the two actions fall under the same statute of the law?

Think of the laws that existed in these two medieval kingdoms in the Caucasus.

Incident one: Cat kills the fly.
Incident two: Dog kills the cat.
Incident three: Cat owner kills the dog.
Incident four: Dog owner kills the cat owner.

Incident five: Valley village men kill the dog owner.
Incident six: Villagers from mountains attack the valley villagers across the border.
Incident seven: The Valley king attacks the Mountain kingdom.
Incident eight: The Mountain king pushes back and starts a full-scale war.

Question 2:

Can you separate these actions based on a) animal instinct; b) human crimes; c) possible acts that may not qualify as crime by medieval laws but contain intent to hurt someone?

Question 3:

At what point was it easier to stop the aggravation?

Question 4:

What kind of modern laws mitigate these types of aggravations? Think of local laws, international laws, city ordinances, sanitary rules and regulations, and so on.

Question 5:

Do you think your village, town, or country needs any additional laws to mitigate these types of aggravation?

This exercise does not include provided answers at the end of the book because there can be multiple valid interpretations. The

Lesson 5: Withhold Your Initial Reaction

name of this lesson is 'Withhold Your Initial Reaction.' This is something we cannot hold animals responsible for—we can only restrain them from further action—but as human beings, we have the ability to withhold our initial reactions. Doing so helps prevent unnecessary conflicts. Understanding culpability ensures that victims are not wrongly blamed, while recognizing intent to harm allows us to distinguish between accidental harm and malicious intent. Ultimately, withholding our initial reactions fosters healthier interpersonal and societal relationships.

LESSON 6: ASSUME GOOD INTENT

In Lesson 3, we discussed the importance of asking questions instead of making blatant assumptions. In Lesson 5, we discussed the importance of withholding your urge for immediate reaction when you are placed in a defensive position. In Lesson 5, we also discussed the potential for damage when the urge to react escalates to its maximum. Now let's discuss what questions to ask once you tame your urge to react.

Although I can't repeat enough the importance of looking into the situation without any assumptions, there is one exception. There is one assumption that we can start with, in order to craft the questions correctly: good intent.

The first question that comes to mind is "Good for whom?" Hopefully, this would be good for both parties, but first of all good for the person who acted first and now you are reacting to their action. Think of it as the following chain of thoughts to your initial reaction: "Is this person attacking me? Is this person trying to hurt me?" (Here, remember that you need to withhold your initial urge to react and to keep thinking.) "Maybe the reason for this action is not to hurt me, but rather, they are acting with good intent. Good for whom? For themselves, at least."

Even if the intent might not be good for you, good for them is better than bad for you. When you assume bad intent, there is no room for negotiations. *This person is going to hurt me. I need to either hide or fight back.* When you assume good intent, even if it is not necessarily good for you but at least good for the attacker, there is room for negotiation. Maybe there is a way to find a solution that is good for both of you. Maybe you can brainstorm that solution together.

So, assuming good intent helps you to cool down and think more rationally. This is just an initial assumption that creates some space for you to think of follow up questions. Because in Lesson 3 we learned to "Ask, not assume!" You only start from your initial assumption of good intent, but you can't stay there. You need to ask questions to collect facts and understand the situation. The more you understand, the better you will be able to negotiate.

The legal term for assuming good intent is "giving someone the benefit of the doubt." The main difference between these two terms is the starting point. When you start from assuming a good intent, you start from a positive, trusting mindset.

When you start from giving someone the benefit of the doubt, you try to overcome your mistrust and suspicion to choose the trust.

Because we are discussing how to craft more efficient questions, starting from an open mindset is important. That is why assuming good intent is a better term for our purposes.

Exercise 6.1 — Withhold Your Reaction

Remember the mother with two children fighting over the orange in Lesson 3? What ideas might have gone through the mother's head? What if she had a headache and their noise over the orange amplified her headache? Is it possible that the first idea that went through her head was: "Those kids will drive me crazy?" or "The kids are fighting deliberately to amplify my headache!" What kind of mind exercise do you think she went through in order to come up with the question, "Why do you need the orange?" Can you write a scenario with a possible chain of thoughts that lead from "They drive me crazy!" to "Why do you need the orange?" What step do you think she undertook in between to come up with her final question?

Exercise 6.2 — The Meeting of Mice (adapted from Atabek Khnkoyan's poem)

The chief mouse called a meeting of all mice living nearby. There was only one item on the agenda: who would hang a bell on the cat's neck? The chief mouse started his speech by describing the dreadful situation and the cat's urge to destroy their clan. He showed the bell that he had brought with him and proclaimed: "What a safe world it would be if this bell was hanging on the cat's neck!" He suggested that two of the mice could hold the cat by his back legs, and one of them could climb onto his head in order to hang the bell on the cat's neck. He assigned three mice that he thought would be the best to fulfill the task. The three mice disagreed and pointed fingers at other mice from the neighborhood that would better fit the job description. Finally, one mouse suggested that the chief mouse should undertake the task himself, since it was his idea in the first place. The chief mouse refused, claiming that it was his job to make speeches and not to hang bells. The meeting ended with no resolution.

Question 1:

If the mice started their meeting assuming good intent, and assuming that the cat's main goal was not necessarily to annihilate their clan but perhaps for some other benefit, what would that be? Can you think of a reason why a cat might eat mice, other than to annihilate the mice clan?

Question 2:

If the mice started with assuming good intent and conducted a brainstorming session, what ideas do you think they would suggest, other than hanging a bell?

LESSON 7: VERIFY YOUR ASSUMPTION

"Negative focus keeps you stuck. The appreciative mindset frees you up!"

— JACQUELINE KELM

Although assuming good intent is a good starting point, we still need to verify our assumptions. In order to verify them, we need to ask the right questions to collect relevant information. In Lesson 4 we discussed Fran Peavey's method of strategic questioning for helping a team member to come up with their own solution. We also discussed the importance of asking the question "why" five times in a row for self-exploration that digs deeper.

Now let's discuss the questions that you need to pose to others in order to collect valid information and verify your assumptions. (Knowing that some of your assumptions could be wrong and you will need to replace them with correct information.) You can still ask several "why"s to dig deeper. You still can ask Level-1 and Level-2 questions to understand the situation.

You can ask open-ended questions. You can ask multiple-choice questions to collect and analyze statistical data. However, there is one more ingredient that makes people open up, participate, and feel more engaged. These are the questions with an appreciative mindset.

A Half-Cup of Water

"Is this cup half-full or half-empty?" Consider changing this question:

"What are the three best qualities of the water that you see in this cup?"

Is the second question manipulative? Yes: you are interested in collecting only information about water. You are not interested in measuring the emptiness in that cup. So, if you are a team leader, tasked to fill up this cup with water, it is the water that you are interested in discussing.

Can the more open question "what do you see in this cup" be more relevant? It is a more open-ended question and less manipulative. It is a useful question when you try to understand what type of personality you are dealing with.

However, let's assume that in this situation you already have the team members you are assigned to work with. You are not tasked with selecting personnel. You have been tasked with filling up the cup with a team that has already been selected. So, in this situation you need to motivate your team members. Therefore, you collect your team members' preferences regarding water. What do they like about water? Why do they like it? What are the best memories they have from the time when that cup was full with water? Water in this example is something positive, so you start with appreciating that positive.

PART II
THE POWER OF APPRECIATION

LESSON 8: THE PRINCIPLES OF APPRECIATIVE INQUIRY

1. Constructionist Principle
2. Simultaneity Principle
3. Poetic Principle
4. Anticipatory Principle
5. Positivity Principle (3, 8)

The principles of Appreciative Inquiry are very similar to the principles of proposal development or project management. To implement any project, you need to set your goals, assess your resources, and assign people, time, and money. You also will need to create a monitoring and evaluation plan to assess your progress at each step. The difference between regular project management and a management based on Appreciative Inquiry is the fact that you walk through each step with an appreciative mindset.

The first step, assessing your positive assets, is called the *Constructionis*t Principle. It is based on the assumption that there is always something positive possible to identify in any situation. If it is a grave situation or a loss, then, at least you have the knowledge of what had happened. You learned a lesson or you are able to share a dear memory of someone you lost.

The second step is based on the *Simultaneity* Principle: if you see something positive, say something positive. The minute you notice something positive, ask your question in a way that redirects everyone's attention to that positive. In other words, on the supply-side, supply with positivity in order to trigger a demand for positivity on the demand-side. The assumption here is that listeners will appreciate the subject of your inquiry simultaneously with you asking your questions in an appreciative way.

The next step is allowing everyone on your team to find in that topic something that they appreciate the most. This is called the *Poetic* Principle since there is more than one way to appreciate things. To summarise all three principles, once you have identified the positive aspect, and asked your team members about the topic of interest in an appreciative way, then expect them to appreciate it in their own way, which may be different from what you appreciated the most. This principle is very important for motivating your team members, as it allows each of them to find something that appeals to them.

Once you determine who likes what, you can assign roles and responsibilities based on what each team member likes doing the most. You have to envision something that incorporates the majority's dreams and desires. Envisioning keeps the motivation alive. This step is done based on the *Anticipatory* Principle where each team member anticipates something positive. Monitoring and Evaluation is a project implementation tool that measures the success of implementation. The *Anticipatory* principle suggests to use this tool in a positive way at each step of project implementation.

Finally, the last step is coordinating between the work of various parts, making sure that the entire project altogether moves in a positive way. This last step is called the *Positivity* Principle. Although we may have tried our best to make sure that each step of this process was positive for each team member, we also want to have a bird's eye view to make sure that overall the project is moving in the right direction. The Positivity Principle is the ability to zoom in and zoom out to make sure that all parts of the mechanism are moving in a positive direction.

If we use our half-cup water example, the *Constructionist* Principle is the ability to see that there is water in that cup. The *Simultaneity* Principle is the team leader's ability to ask the question in a way that the rest of the team notices that water. "What are the best three qualities of the water you see in that cup?" The *Poetic* Principle is the team leader's ability to accept that different people may like different things about water. Instead of assuming that everyone will say "water quenches my thirst," the Appreciative Inquiry practitioner is able to hear that someone appreciates water because when the weather is hot and the water in that cup is icy cold, they can put the cold icy bottom of that cup on their eyes and let their eyes rest. At the same time, someone else may appreciate a hot half-cup of water in the middle of winter to warm up their hands.

In the world of virtual meetings and global projects, people gathered in the same virtual space may be from different time zones and experience different weather conditions. The more ideas you gather, the more complex solutions you can create. The *Anticipatory* Principle guides you towards creating a collective vision that incorporates most of the ideas and is as inclusive as possible. It also encourages you to dream big. The *positive* principle makes sure that whatever vision you created collectively is implemented to give the desired result. Dreaming big is combined with making specific, measurable, achievable, realistic, and time-bound (SMART) steps to climb towards that big dream.

The five principles listed above are the classic principles of Appreciative Inquiry outlined by David Cooperrider, the founder of Appreciative Inquiry. Many other followers of the idea of positive psychology have applied them to various spheres of our lives, created their own theories, given different names to these principles, aligned those names to a specific letter of the alphabet, subdivided some principles into sub-principles, suggested brand new principles etc. However, the main idea is the same: if you want to give something a positive spin, make sure that each step of your actions involves moving in a positive direction as much as possible. The following five chapters will be based on Jacqueline Kelm's interpretation of all five principles of Appreciative Inquiry.

Exercise 8.1 — Find a positive topic

Below is a list of 10 negative topics. Follow the examples below and flip the rest of the topics into positive.

Negative: Anti-Corruption Committee
Positive: Ethics Committee

Negative: Combating Environmental Pollution
Positive: Advancing Clean and Sustainable Environments

Negative: Resistance of Materials
Positive: Strength of Materials

Continue on your own:

Lesson 8: The Principles of Appreciative Inquiry

Negative: Reducing Energy Waste
Positive:

Negative: Eliminating Customer Complaints
Positive:

Negative: Preventing System Downtime
Positive:

Negative: Decreasing Unemployment Rates
Positive:

Negative: Limiting Traffic Accidents
Positive:

Negative: Addressing Poor Academic Performance
Positive:

Negative: Reducing Food Waste
Positive:

Negative: Avoiding Financial Losses
Positive:

Negative: Stopping Cybersecurity Breaches
Positive:

Negative: Reducing Water Shortages
Positive:

(Suggested answers are provided in Appendix A to facilitate discussion and reflection.)

LESSON 9: CONSTRUCTIONIST PRINCIPLE

There are many interpretations of the five principles of Appreciative Inquiry as defined by David Cooperrider. We will discuss those principles based on Jaqcueline Kelm's interpretation in her book "The Joy of Appreciative Living." (1,13-22)

Jacqueline Kelm's 5 Commandments of the Constructionist Principle.

1. We live in the world our stories create;
2. Change your stories to change your life;
3. Accept the bad while deliberately looking for the inherent strengths, gifts, and positive possibilities;
4. See the best in others without being blind to their weaknesses;
5. Note where we don't have control and move to where we have control.

One of the most important aspects of the Constructionist

Principle is understanding that the ability to note something good does not mean ignoring the negative aspects of the problem. It simply means to look at it, acknowledge it, and move beyond it towards the solution. The difference between constructive feedback and harsh criticism is in the effort to look deliberately for strengths.

Giving Constructive Feedback

The formula of constructive feedback is very simple:

1. Describe what you like.
2. Suggest what could be improved.
3. Suggest how to do this.

Based on the Constructionist Principle, there is always a way to find something that you liked or appreciated. What if you didn't like the result? You still may mention that there was a certain thought put into the process. You still may appreciate the time and the courage that it took for that person to come to you and seek your feedback. So, if you don't like the results or consider the effort made was insufficient, you may try finding something positive outside of that box: the reason this person was assigned to do this work, the good results they've had in the past, etc. If nothing else comes to your mind, try to state what you would like to see instead rather than what isn't working for you.

Renowned management consultant Peter Drucker, in an interview with David Cooperrider, said that a leader's job is to make the strengths of people effective and their weaknesses irrelevant. You might need to note the weaknesses in order to make them irrelevant. But when you think about putting together a team effort, do you really start from thinking about the weaknesses of each team member, or do you concentrate on what needs to be done and who can do it the best? If you look deliberately for the strengths and make an effort to assign to every task the most suitable candidate, you will spend less time analyzing irrelevant tasks. So, the strength-based approach is deliberate to a point but it becomes a part of participants' second nature once you figure out together the best working mechanism.

What if you are not the boss and therefore not in charge of assigning roles? First of all, giving feedback is also a leadership skill; you do not need to be the boss in order to demonstrate good leadership skills and provide good feedback. Second, if you are well-versed in the assertive style of communication, maximally respectful and polite, you can say anything that you need to tell to your friends, co-workers, and even your boss, if you focus on how to improve team effort.

Finally, if your co-worker is not well versed in sharing constructive feedback and gives you harsh criticism, your ability to look deliberately for positive possibilities should help you to take from those harsh words only the parts that help you to improve, and consider the harshness irrelevant to your task of improving your performance.

Have you heard the following poem, often used during support-group meetings?
They address a need for:
1. The serenity to accept the things I cannot change;
2. The courage to change the things I can; and
3. The wisdom to know the difference."

Jacqueline Kelm suggests reframing the Serenity prayer in the following way:

"Grant me:
1. The serenity to accept the people I can not change,
2. The courage to change the one I can, and
3. The wisdom to know it's me." (1,19)

In other words, any action–reaction combination has necessary and sufficient conditions for success. The moment you realize that the power of changing yourself is entirely in your hands, you can concentrate on supplying the necessary conditions for your success and minimizing your dependency on anyone else. Thus, you have the power to provide 100% of what is necessary for your success, with 0% need for sufficient conditions provided by others: changing anyone other than you becomes irrelevant.

But what if this is a group effort and, while doing your best is necessary, it is not sufficient for the collective success because others need to do their part of work? This is when your ability to stay positive and give constructive feedback becomes so important. If you start with assuming good intent, talking in a polite and respectful way with your teammates about what has worked and what is needed, asking them to help find a collective solution, the chances are that you may come up with something workable for all of you. But if you have tried and it has not worked, if you have realised that your assumption of good intent was wrong, or their intent was good but they are lacking the skills you need, your next step is not changing that person, but re-assessing the pool of strengths and asking for help from those who can help. In this situation, the wisdom to know that you are the only person whom you can change tells you that you have control over your action to ask for additional help, find allies, go to your boss' boss, further define your job description, or change your work, etc. Whatever solution comes to you, it should be based on assessing your strengths and appreciating your time and effort. Changing someone else who does not want to or cannot change remains inefficient and unsustainable.

Stalinism

Going behind the back of your co-worker and complaining to their boss has the potential of growing into something ugly. Stalinism is the ugliest form it can grow into, when co-workers write anonymous accusations in order to get the victim's job, or neighbors write anonymous accusations in order to acquire the victim's apartment. This happens when the power is concentrated in the hands of the executive officials while courts and legislation do only what the executive branch dictates. No matter how much I am a proponent of assertive communication, there might be times when passive or passive–aggressive forms of communication may save your life. Even in these situations, you should be able to ask yourself: am I doing this to save my life or to get someone else into trouble and gain from it? While being passive or doing something in order to save your own life is a gray area that I can not comment on, doing so deliberately to get someone else into trouble is not a reason to justify your job promotion or new asset. This is when intent to harm becomes a decision-making factor. The only control that you have over this situation might be that you have the ability not to do harm.

Example:

Laura was a young accountant in 1937 when her father was arrested by Stalin's regime and taken away. There were neither formal charges nor a court hearing scheduled; he was simply taken away from home one day. He never returned.

Lesson 9: Constructionist Principle

Laura was working in a state agency with a very old and experienced chief accountant who was her mentor. One day the chief accountant took the abacus and stated:

"During the Tzar's time the purchasing power of one ruble was:

- Three kilograms of potatoes (she slid 3 beads on the abacus); or
- Two dozen eggs (she slid back the 3 beads and put instead 2 beads for 10, and 4 for single units); or
- A kilo of beef.

What can we purchase now with the Soviet ruble? Only:

- One kilogram of potatoes,
- A dozen eggs, or
- 400 grams of meat.

And they are trying to say there is no inflation? Here is the mathematical proof!"

An hour later Laura was invited to the political management office for interrogation.

"What was the Chief Accountant saying an hour ago? We heard there was a conversation about the Tzar's ruble, the new ruble, and inflation."

"The chief accountant was saying that during the Tzar time the purchasing power of his ruble was:

- Only a kilo of potatoes, or
- A dozen of eggs, or
- 400 grams of meat

But with today's ruble we can buy:

- Three kilograms of potatoes,
- Two dozen of eggs,
- And a kilo of beef!"

Laura was sliding the beads on the abacus in the interrogation room, like the Chief Accountant had done.

"Our enemies are trying to say that we have inflation? No, there is none. Here is the mathematical proof!"

Laura solemnly pushed the abacus towards her interrogators. They let her go and never questioned her or the chief accountant about the incident.

In this example Laura saved two lives, the Chief Accountant's and her own, by being untruthful. She used a passive–aggressive style of communication. She reframed something negative into something positive and allowed the leadership to have peace of mind and probably report a success story about their political propaganda work. She took a risk, because there was a chance the political leadership had planted the Chief Accountant's strange conversation to frame her. They had already arrested her father; there was a chance that now the same people were going after her. But she started from assuming that probably the Chief Accountant's intent was good. She knew the person as her mentor. She had learned a lot from her mentor and appreciated all of the knowledge and the fun they had together at work. The Chief Accountant was representing the older generation who said whatever they thought.

She also assumed good intent on the part of the political leadership. They were just doing their job. They had fragments of the conversation. Probably someone else had mentioned something that they had overheard, so the leadership had to react and verify the information. Then Laura asked herself, *what if my assumptions are wrong*? If her assumptions were wrong and the political leadership was after her, they would arrest her no matter what her response was. There was a front page article in the newspapers in those days: "The child is not responsible for the deeds of his father." Based on this article, many children of arrested parents were allowed to return back to work or university, even if they had been removed from work and school after their parent's arrest. The assumption of good intent on the part of political leadership had some factual grounds, even though the environment was volatile.

The bottom line was if she told the truth, she would hurt two people: herself and her mentor. If she lied, she would save the mentor and still could claim that was how she had understood the mentor's words. So she acted in self-defense and followed the concept of "do not harm."

Exercise 9.1 — Start with "Yes"

Ask a group member a question that requires a "yes" or "no" response. Do you have a brother? Do you like milk? Are you a doctor? Etc. If you know the person, try to ask questions with the answer "no." For example, if you know the person has only a brother, ask them if they have a sister. If you know the person hates milk in his coffee, ask if they would like some coffee with plenty of room for milk.

The other person's task is to give a true and correct answer but start their response with the word "yes." For example, if the person has no sister and the question is "Do you have a sister," the answer should be, "Yes, I always wanted to have one, but I only have a brother." The point of the exercise is to find something that you can agree with, but still tell the truth. If you say "yes, I have a sister" that would be a lie. If you say "no, I don't have a sister", that would be a true answer but still wrong for the purpose of this exercise because you did not make any effort to connect with the inquirer and to agree on something. The rule of the game is to start with "yes" but answer truthfully.

Exercise 9.2 — Ability to Reframe

Arrange groups of 4–5 people. List several problems that you are currently experiencing in your life, at school, at work, at home, or with your friends. For example, "the training at work was boring," "making us learn math is stupid," etc. Just be yourself and state the problems that bother you, but make sure to be decent and respectful.

Once you have a good pool of problems, take turns and randomly select a problem. Read the problem in your mind and flip it out loud. In other words, instead of reading directly what problem is written, say what would you like instead or what you wish you had. For example: "The training should be more interactive," or "We should study more elective subjects at school." and so on.

LESSON 10: SIMULTANEITY PRINCIPLE

Jacqueline Kelm's 4 Commandments of Simultaneity Principle:

1. Change begins simultaneously in the moment we ask the question;
2. The questions we ask have the power to shift our focus;
3. It is not about asking the right questions, but asking the questions that take us to the right direction (which is any place that is better than the current place);
4. What do I want more of in this situation? What gives life? The trick is to get clear about what we want in order to create it. (1, 37-49)

Reframing the Problem

In Exercise 9.2, we tried to flip the problem into what we would like to have instead. This allowed the person who wrote the problem to see it from another angle and hopefully gave them another perspective. We can take one more step to make the process of reframing more efficient. We can elevate the reframed topic to make it more exciting and attractive for the listener.

For example:

Step One, Define the problem: The training was boring.
Step Two, Reframe it: The training should be more interesting.
Step Three, Elevate it to create more excitement: Creating engaging and interactive training sessions that we love to attend.

Here are a couple of more examples:

Step 1: School lunches are bland and unappealing.
Step 2: School lunches should be tastier.
Step 3: Create delicious and nutritious school lunches that everyone looks forward to.

Step 1: Group projects are frustrating because some people don't contribute.
Step 2: Group projects should have better teamwork.
Step 3: Designing group projects that spark collaboration and shared success.

Exercise 10.1 — Reframe and Elevate

Continue with the pool of problems that you created in Exercise 9.2 and go through the three-step process.

How to make the reframed topic more exciting?

In order to understand how to make the topics more exciting, let's first understand why we are doing this. Based on the Simultaneity Principle, the moment we pose a more intriguing question, we increase the probability that our listener is interested in continuing the dialogue. So, adding excitement helps the respondent to become a more active listener. It helps your audience to interact, participate, and get engaged. If you are facilitating a group, it helps to create a secure environment where everyone is willing to share their ideas and experiences, and therefore contribute to the collective knowledge. There are several rules for the facilitator, such as: 1) share air, 2) agree to disagree, 3) withhold negative facial expressions, 4) make it more inclusive, etc. But these are the next steps necessary to maintain the secure environment created. The very first step is, however, to break the ice of silence and help the participants to find the courage to participate. This is done better if the facilitator takes time to think in advance about a single topic that can interest and connect with everyone.

Example:

Back in 2003, a Vermont-based non-profit agency was implementing a USAID-supported Community Connections Project. Within the framework of that project, educators from various former Soviet Republics were visiting the USA, meeting American educators, observing classes, and sharing experiences. In one of these meetings a group of school teachers from Armenia and a group from Azerbaijan met at the School for International Training in Vermont for a workshop on Peace Building. At the time, the countries were in a stage of a decade-long active war.

The facilitator asked: "Think back to a time when there was peace and you lived peacefully next to each other. What did you appreciate the most in your neighbor?"

"Can't we discuss this topic in the example of the relationship between Israel and Palestine?" asked the participants.

There was a certain resistance to discussing the elephant in the room; they would rather have talked about their relationship through indirect parallels with Israel–Palestine relations. This resistance was because they were not feeling that they were in an environment where it was safe to discuss difficult problems.

In this case, the facilitator went through step one and defined the problem as war. He also went through step two, and reframed it into peace. What do you think step three should have been? How could you make the topic more attractive for this specific audience?

Often, it is helpful to divide participants into groups of two or three people and ask them to share some personal stories with each other. It helps if you know about their professional interests or things that they are compassionate about. In this case, all the participants were school teachers. So maybe, to break the ice, the facilitator could have asked:

"Think of the time when you decided to become a school teacher. What was the reason you selected that path? What is the most rewarding experience you have had as a school teacher? Share with your partner your personal story." This type of question has a higher probability of encouraging the representatives from two opposing sides to enter into a dialogue with each other.

The key words to everything that we discuss here is "a higher probability." We can not guarantee that it will work, but we can try our best to increase the probability of success. After all, trying our best is within our control.

On a simpler note, if you want your three-year-old to eat

their food or put on their socks and you know that their favorite answer is "no," how would you elevate the topic to make it sound more exciting?

"Would you like to eat your soup with croutons or with a slice of bread?"
"Would you like to put on socks with elephants or socks with turtles?"

While there is a chance that the answer will be "neither," you have offered a choice and they are now thinking about the choice rather than how soon they can give you their favorite answer, "no." So, you have increased your probability of receiving a response other than "no." It might not necessarily be the response you want, but there is more room for negotiations because you have offered more choices.

Whenever we touch on the topic of more than one choice, we are ready to discuss the Poetic Principle. However, before we move on to that principle, there is one more secret of elevating the reframed topic to make it more exciting.

Changing Object with Subject

Often, when you start exploring various leadership styles, you think of yourself, or your organization, or your country as the one who delivers aid or services, and you have a target group that is the recipient. Try to change that approach. Try to think of that target group as being in charge of the initiative and see if you or the donor agency can benefit from it as a recipient.

Example:

> Step One: A group of forcibly displaced people are having a hard time navigating the difficulties of new life after immigrating to a new country.
> Step Two: Integrating the group of forcibly displaced people into the new society.
> Step Three: Learning the wisdom and resilience from the group of forcibly displaced people to enrich the society they are now part of.

Once you start treating your target group as a subject rather than object, you indicate that they are your equal partner and you can learn from each other, even when their experience was bad.

Here are a couple more examples:

> Step One: Students are struggling to adapt to the challenging curriculum.
> Step Two: Supporting students to better navigate the curriculum.
> Step Three: Discovering how student perspectives can guide curriculum improvement and make learning more engaging.

> Step One: Diverse employees feel excluded in traditional workplace cultures.
> Step Two: Creating inclusive spaces where diverse employees feel welcomed.
> Step Three: Allowing diverse employees to shape a richer, more innovative workplace culture.

Lesson 10: Simultaneity Principle

This technique highlights how shifting the perspective to involve the subject in shaping solutions creates opportunities for empowerment, inclusion, and innovation.

Exercise 10.2 — Elevate the Topic

Hopefully, at this point you are ready to drop the first step and start directly from a reframed perspective. Continue the idea of shifting the target group from the recipient to the empowered active participant.

Step Two: Improving public transportation to serve commuters better.
Step Three:

Step Two: Encouraging teenagers to participate in civic activities.
Step Three:

Step Two: Helping local communities adapt to environmental challenges.
Step Three:

Continue with the topics you reframed in Exercise 10.1

(Suggested answers are provided in Appendix A to facilitate discussion and reflection.)

James F. Finckenauer's Theory of Legal Socialization.

A prominent American criminologist, James F. Finckenauer, divides societies into three levels:

Level 1: Law-obeying society. This is the society where members obey the law because they are afraid of punishment (if they break the law).

Level 2: Law-maintaining society. This is the society where the majority of members follow the rules because they think it is the right thing to do. (There are, of course, also the members who obey the law because they are afraid of consequences.)

Level 3: Law-making society. This is the society where not only do the members obey and maintain the law, but many of them actively participate in making the law.

Law-making societies are characterized by their active engagement in creating, amending, and evolving legal systems to address changing social, economic, and cultural needs. (7)

Characteristics:

- Dynamic Legal Frameworks: Laws are regularly revisited, revised, or replaced in response to societal feedback and changing circumstances.
- Participatory Processes: Citizens often play a role in shaping laws through voting, public consultations, or activism.
- Innovation and Progress: Legal systems are seen as tools for addressing inequality, injustice, or emerging societal challenges.
- Challenge to Authority: Legal and social reform

movements may challenge traditional norms and structures, driving the creation of new laws.

This model is also used in the theory of education, where the educators are trying to create a learning environment where students study, not because they are afraid of being punished (by low scores), but mostly because they enjoy studying and actively participate in shaping their learning environment.

We can use the same approach when we try to reframe the problem into a more appreciative topic. Who are the victims of the problem that we are trying to solve? Can we reframe the problem in such a way that the beneficiaries are empowered to actively participate in the solution?

LESSON 11: POETIC PRINCIPLE

Jacqueline Kelm's 5 Commandments of Poetic Principle:

1. We can find whatever we want in any situation;
2. Whatever we focus on, becomes a bigger part of our reality;
3. We see what we have learned to see, unless we choose to see beyond it;
4. We have to create new patterns in our thinking to shift our attention to the positive, and this takes intentional effort and practice. (1, 22–36)

In a previous example regarding the half-cup of water, I elevated the reframed topic and then added a random number to it: "What are the three best qualities of the water that you see in this cup?"

Why do you think I added number three?

Well, first of all, I wanted the respondents to see that water possesses more than one good quality. I wanted them to get unstuck from the fact that "water quenches thirst," move beyond that, and recognize some other qualities. Also, I wanted to make sure that people were not repeating the same response. Once they have heard three different responses, the chances are they may come up with new ideas. Three is a philosophical number, with many things happening three times. For some religions, three is a holy number. The number three helps to define borders: this is too much, this is too little, and this is the "Goldilocks zone". When you create a system of checks and balances, three works better than two, because it can side with one of the remaining two to create the majority. In other words, if you generate too many ideas, in order to eliminate some, it could be easier to pick one out of three rather than one out of two (that is, "this one is definitely no, this one is a maybe, this one is a bit more than a maybe"). Newton's method of gradual approximation is based on numerous iterations between groups of three numbers. (Again, according to the same principle, these two are the borders and we target the middle that becomes the border for the next group of three.) In digital marketing, three options, or three radio buttons on the screen, are big enough to catch your eye on both a computer screen and a phone screen. Here again, sized equally, they have the same probability of catching your visual attention, and you can gradually redirect that attention to the price you want (this price is too low, this is too expensive, and here is the recommended package).

However, the main purpose of the Poetic Principle is not just to generate ideas, but also to create opportunities for each participant to find the most appealing one for themselves. Because when people like the topic, when they volunteer to champion an effort, they thrive. Therefore, one of the most important tasks of inspirational leadership is to provide opportunities for everyone to find what they like the best.

This is why Jacqueline Kelm keeps saying:

"Negative focus keeps you stuck.
The appreciative mindset frees you up."

When you operate based on fear, you narrow down your options to one: define the target and incapacitate it. It is a very effective strategy if you know for sure that this is the only task that you need to resolve in order to solve the problem. However, when you operate based on strengths, you open your mind and see that there is potentially more than one solution. In fact there are so many of them, that each can pick the one they like the best.

Is the lack of bad news considered good news?

Jackqueline Kelm suggests doing daily appreciation exercises to train your brain to look for the good deliberately (See Exercise 13.1). Based on her explanation, our brain creates new neurological connections to think more positively. It takes about 28 days to grow new neurons; sometimes, you have to force yourself to list three good things that you appreciated during that day. It gets even harder to do when, as she suggests, to list new things each time. In some other models, they suggest trying to list five different things every day. In my childhood we had "train games," the games we used on long train rides, where you had to list 50 uses for a chair, for example. The Program *Odyssey of the Mind* (12) often uses exercises where a line of kids quickly says, one after the other, how to use a given object in some extraordinary conditions (For example: "Imagine this hat is the size of this room. What could you do with it?" The kids quickly start listing possibilities: park an airplane in it. Jump on the roof like on a trampoline. Put googly eyes, and so on.) There is a huge range of improv warm up exercises available on YouTube.

So, if you are stuck, if you have a hard time listing three different good things that you appreciate in your life, it is OK to say once, "at least nothing bad happened today." Or if something bad happened, to say, "it could have been worse, I'm thankful for it not being the worst case scenario." These ideas are better than nothing. But if you get stuck and use the same trick over and over again, you are not opening up your mind to see the good next to the bad. You are still stuck on excluding the bad from your day's routine.

So, the answer to the question in this section is yes, the lack of bad news is indeed good news, but avoid overusing it. This single idea is not sufficient for you to create new neurological connections in your brain and come up with new thinking patterns. It is only useful if you need to calm yourself down and withhold your reaction. Make a step beyond it. Look around your room, pick any object on your desk or your wall, and think of three things you appreciate about that object. If you would rather have a more challenging exercise to develop creativity, use improv warm ups, they can be a lot of fun.

Does the Expression "Fake it till you make it" work?

In Lesson 9, when we were discussing Stalinism in the example about Laura and her mentor, she faked it and she made it. So, yes, the expression "fake it till you make it" has a certain truth to it because you need to put an effort into something before you reach the desired result. However, if you make a sincere effort, you might be able to reach that result much faster. Sometimes you need to listen to a piece of classical music, for example, many times until you develop a taste for it. Sometimes you need to try a new food several times until you decide that you like it. You don't have to lie and say, "oh this music is so beautiful" if you don't see the beauty in it. You can simply say that you are giving it a try since so many people have recommended it. So, there is a way to stay sincere and truthful to yourself, but continue working on building a new thinking pattern.

When I was little, my parents hired a music teacher to prepare me for a music school admission exam. I failed at the first attempt so, for a year, the teacher would play a note on the piano and I was supposed to sing the same pitch. Sometimes I got it right. Other times I sang a wrong note. One day she said:

> "You are singing in a hurry. You want to repeat the note so fast that you forget to listen to it. Imagine there is a little copy of you inside of you, holding a tiny bell in her hand. When I play the key, wait for that little person in your head to ring that bell, and then sing."

This advice helped. When I worked as a sales assistant in a store during my university years, I was expected to smile at each customer. I had two choices: either put a fake smile on my face or wait for that 'little me' inside to ring that little bell and tell me that this customer deserved a genuine smile. I could look into their eyes, find something that I could connect with—and then smile. At some point, no matter how tired, upset, or hungry I was, that little store was my meditation place. As soon as I entered that space, it was like teleporting into another world where you are nice to people and they are sincerely grateful to you for that.

Take your time to find that inner you. If you are doing your daily appreciation exercise and you run out of ideas, look around, find a little fly on your window rubbing its front legs. Ask that inner you if there anything that you could appreciate about this fly? Wait for that little inner you to send you back her message: "The fly is washing its hands and singing the 'Happy Birthday' song." Or perhaps some other message that you can connect with. Then try to appreciate that connection, or a memory that came with that connection. This way you will learn to appreciate the little moments that help you to make it, without faking it.

Exercise 11.1 — Find Something Nice

I read about this exercise in *Parents* magazine from one of the moms responding to the question of how to explain to your children that, although they've already been given the same thing by someone else, they must say "thank you" politely without letting on that they already have one. This is especially important when they argue that you have said that they should always tell the truth. So, this mom came up with a fun game which I suggest. You have to play this with a child. If you don't have a child in your household, play it with a fellow training participant. You can also do it alone and pretend that you are talking to someone else, but this way you will not learn the second person's perspective.

Make a pile of your gifts from last year, wrap them in kitchen towels (pretend the towel is a gift wrapping paper). Then, pretending that you just received these gifts, open them one by one and thank your playmate (or the imaginary gift-giver) for each gift. You have to find one nice thing about each gift: the color, the texture, the practicality, etc.—everything except the fact that you already have that item. If you can't find anything good about that gift, at least thank the person for their thoughtfulness, time, or effort. If you are playing with a real child, sneak a new gift into the pile and use real wrapping paper.

LESSON 12: ANTICIPATORY PRINCIPLE

Jacqueline Kelm's 4 Commandments of the Anticipatory Principle:

1. The images we anticipate in our minds about the future can influence the future.
2. The actions we need to take to reach our dreams become pretty clear once we figure out where we want to go.
3. Make time to intentionally think about your dream.
4. The better we feel, the better we think. (1, 50–67)

In the first three principles of Appreciative Inquiry (Constructionist, Simultaneity, and Poetic) we were working on the following skills: 1) an ability to discover the positive, 2) an ability to reframe the picture in a way that it inspires others, and 3) an ability to acknowledge that others may see the positive differently than you do.

In other words, we were assessing all the assets we have to work with. Similar to a math task (i.e. a train departed from point A to point B…), we were reading the conditions listed in a task and drawing point A and point B, putting the given conditions on the diagram, indicating a little arrow for the direction and speed of the train, etc. We were creating an inventory of our resources: anything given and appreciated by many in many different ways.

Having listed the assets that we have, now is the time to pose the question – what is the unknown that we are trying to solve? In this chapter we will discuss where we want to go. In the next chapter we will add ideas about how to get there.

The Anticipatory Principle in Appreciative Inquiry is, first of all, an appeal to dream big. As in Simultaneity Principle we were posing an inspirational question to encourage participation, now we are collecting as many ideas as possible without limitations so that people feel that their voices are heard and their desires are recognized. The main rule of the game at this stage is: all ideas are good, and all of them will be listed in exactly the way people suggest them, without filters and censorship. (The rule "be decent" still applies.)

At some point we will sort those ideas, combine some of them, put them in groups, send some of them to a "parking lot" for ideas and so on. We will do everything that is necessary in order to make implementation manageable within the resources we have. But that will be the next step.

Now is the time to think big. Not only think big but also visualize it. Get creative. Write a rap song about it. Make a community mural. Create a bubble gum mosaic and then pour olive oil on it. Write a new title sequence for Phineas and Ferb. You name it. It is your time to shine.

Dreaming big is the cornerstone of the Anticipatory Principle because we allow ourselves to think beyond current limitations. We unlock new possibilities that might otherwise remain hidden. It encourages us to envision outcomes that might seem impossible, but can inspire innovative solutions. Big dreams generate excitement and enthusiasm. When people see the potential for a brighter future, they become more committed and motivated to work toward that vision.

Example

My friend's three-year-old niece was hospitalized with a viral infection. The child was living with her parents in a different country. The doctors in that country put the niece into an artificial coma, hoping that her body would fight the virus while it ran its course. Her condition was not worsening but three days was a long time for the family to wait. Anxiety, sleepless nights, inability to make a call at a certain time to a different time zone were making things more complicated.

At one point my friend became so frustrated that she started complaining about the child's grandmother, who was talking about the child in past tense. "She was such a nice kid!" "She was so much fun." The child was alive, her condition was not worsening. There was still a chance she would recover, but a lot depended on how well her body could fight the infection.

At that point I remembered a parent saying (also in the same *Parents* magazine article) that in these situations it helps to imagine your child as a grownup. Without asking what that three-year-old wants to become or which school she would choose, I jumped into a farthest future that I could think of at that point:

What do you think she will buy with her first salary?

This question was so unexpected that my friend stopped complaining. She started thinking of how she could help from the USA. (Other than sending money.) She contacted her children's American pediatrician and asked questions about the condition. She learned that the doctors in the USA would use a similar treatment plan in a similar situation and that there were some hospitals using advanced techniques. She made a list of hospitals and started calling them. One of the hospitals was in a country that didn't have a good relationship with the country the child's family lived in. The common border was closed and there was no diplomatic relationship between them. She decided to ignore that and make a phone call to the doctor in the second country. Knowing that doctors are not politicians, she assumed good intent because doctors in all parts of the world have the same mission: to save lives. She talked to that doctor, who was very kind and experienced. She asked the doctor to call the hospital the child was in. The doctors from the two adversarial countries had a phone conversation in which they discussed the situation and the treatment plan. Both doctors appreciated the wisdom and the experience of the colleague from the other country.

I don't know what really helped that child to survive. Maybe her body was strong enough to survive that virus on her own. Maybe she heard in her coma that everybody was trying really hard to help her, and that increased her desire to fight. But I can tell you for sure that imagining your sick child all grown up helps the parent to push themselves to think and act beyond traditional limitations.

One of the dilemmas that many people have is how big should they dream? Does it make sense to dream about something that you know you cannot reach? Isn't it easier to just lower the bar? That was the biggest challenge that I had going through my course of Appreciative Inquiry. Dreaming big is important because you need to know your final destination. It is the lighthouse in the ocean of difficulties that you need to cross. If you know the direction, you will find the strength to get there because you can see the point of destination. You can count on your strength. You will learn to control your breathing. You will learn to turn and lie on your back to float and have a rest. But when the light in that lighthouse is missing, you will put in a lot of effort without knowing which way to swim. You have no idea how much time is left, so counting on your strength would be harder. It is much easier to give up when you do not know your final destination.

When we speak about a collective project, a collective image is something more complex than each individual image. So, when everyone wants to push their own ideas, they tend to push down someone else's, thinking that the level of complexity the others are suggesting is too hard for the entire team to reach.

The most important skill for conducting a successful brainstorming session is the ability to embrace everyone's ideas. Share your dreams with others and let them share their dreams with you. There are certain norms to encouraging participation in a brainstorming session.

Suggested Norms to Encourage Participation

- No idea is too small or too big
- Build on each other's ideas
- Listen actively and with respect
- Be encouraging
- Stay open-minded
- Share air
- Agree to disagree
- Have a "Parking Lot" for ideas that are not related to the brainstorming session

Finally, while it is important to keep the image bright enough as a tool for motivation, having only the image does not replace the hard work that needs to be done to succeed. No matter how much the football players visualize success before the game, that image alone is not sufficient to succeed. You still need to practice and work hard to enjoy the victory. The image is just a tool for motivation to continue hard work.

LESSON 13: POSITIVITY PRINCIPLE

Jacqueline Kelm's 5 Commandments of Positivity Principle.

1. Positive emotion is essential for effective change.
2. It is a gradual process of getting a little bit happier over time. It is not about creating the perfect moment or the absolute best experience, but slowly improving your daily experiences.
3. Learning to enjoy the small moments more is the key to creating an overall upward trend.
4. Good feelings have an upward spiral effect. (1, 68–83)

Once all ideas are collected, it is time to group them and assign various task forces to be in charge of building an implementation plan. This is when you determine what kind of staircase to build in order to reach the level that the group dreamed about. You don't need to lower the final destination but you do need to build a reliable staircase with steps small enough to be achievable by each group member.

Lesson 13: Positivity Principle

You need to consider not just the size of each step but the number of steps in a flight. You need to design enough landing spaces. You need to consider the size of your building and switch to a spiral staircase, or to a ladder, if necessary. By changing parameters you can adjust the staircase to your needs without lowering the level of your final destination.

At a proposal development stage, proposal specialists use the SMART acronym to describe the main features of each step. The steps should be Specific, Measurable, Achievable, Realistic, and Time-bound. The process of design of these steps is smoother when the team members have the opportunity to choose the task force they join themselves. Each person brings their own wisdom, knowledge, and experience to the process, and they know the best how and when to use their set of skills. If there are tasks left without the champions and followers, then the management should assign those tasks or hire the missing specialists. This is when the manager has the opportunity to amplify peoples' strengths and, as Peter Drucker says, make their weaknesses irrelevant.

On an individual level, a child may see a ballet or a concert and dream about becoming a ballerina or a pianist. At that point the child has no idea how much hard work will need to be put in order to become the image they have in their head. When in a year or two they realize how hard it is, the image that the child had could be the only thing that keeps them going. Those who do not have a clear, strong, and compelling image, might quit.

Quitting is also OK. You quit because you still are actively searching for the ideal image for you. Once you figure that image out, you will go and get it. Sometimes you walk because you know where you want to go. Sometimes you walk because you enjoy walking and the destination is not important. Whenever you are confused, use Fran Peavey's Strategic Questioning technique to find clearness. Add to it your ability to reframe your questions in a positive way and elevate them to make them more exciting.

The point is to do what you enjoy doing. If you love your work but it does not pay much, figure out how to get passive sources of income. If your work pays a lot but you always dreamed about doing something else, volunteer for that passion. This is when you try out different flights of stairs and come up with your very own design.

Often we are taught at school that we need to have a plan before we write an essay. Or that, when we start a business, we need to write a business plan before we begin. But there are people for whom the ideas are pouring out, leading one to another. They do not need to write the major talking point first, they just start and one thing leads to another. Then, they may collect feedback and decide which idea impacts others and maybe at that point start thinking of a new production schedule. Some businessmen can start from testing out some new ideas on a small scale. They might try several price strategies before they are ready to create a business plan.

What Appreciative Inquiry is suggesting is that, whatever implementation strategy you choose, do it with joy. If you are a small team trying to start something new but the team members can't agree on which direction to go, start by listening to every suggestion and offering each person to lead a specific effort in an area that they enjoy. Give them the opportunity to lead one effort and promise to be their follower, in exchange for them being your follower in the effort that you are trying to lead. You can try different things, see what combination works best, and then work on creating an Implementation master plan.

Sometimes the staircase might be more like a board game

"Snakes and Ladders." Sometimes you may slide back. Sometimes you find a shortcut. Embrace all of it and enjoy the ride.

In her chapter on the Positivity Principle, Jacqueline Kelm has a diagram showing that the level of joy that you reach over time is similar to the behavior of a financial market things go up and down many times per day. But in order to get an overall upward trend, you need to make sure that every time you are down, you can control your feelings and recuperate a bit more quickly than the previous time, so that you don't feel as badly as you did the last time. For example, if you went through your first heartbreak, were depressed and couldn't leave your room for four months, but you learned that forcing yourself to go out and meet friends would help you to overcome the difficult feelings, the next time you experience heartbreak, you might force yourself to do something rewarding for you in four days rather than four months. Why? Because from that first painful experience you learned what worked. You can appreciate the experience, the new wisdom you learned, and therefore, you are better prepared for the new crisis. You even know how to mitigate things that are within your control.

Sometimes the crises happen again without an opportunity to mitigate. There can be losses and mistakes; there might be accidents or wars. Every time, with every incident, you will get stronger and stronger and you will enrich your skill set of ways to get a little bit happier over time. This can happen if, and only if, you see in each incident both the positive and the negative, but choose to concentrate on the positive to enrich your skill set.

Exercise 13.1 — Jacqueline Kelm's "Exercise of Joy" Practice

"After intentionally practicing Appreciative Inquiry, the brain forms new neurological connections."

— JACQUELINE KELM

Every day email your teacher:

1. Three good things that happened during the day, things for which you are grateful or happy. Choose three different things each time.
2. Add to the email one thing that you plan to experience during the following day with joy, pleasure, or satisfaction. If, the next day, you succeed, you may use the result in the following day's email as one of your accomplishments that day.

Once a week:

- Take 15 min to envision and write about your ideal joy-filled life.

Once a month:

- Make an assessment: "How is your life getting better." (1, 161-170)

LESSON 14: THE MAGIC FORMULA FOR EMPOWERING QUESTIONS

In order to facilitate a brainstorming session and identify the breadth and depth of the issues that need to be encompassed, Appreciative Inquiry practitioners use the following formula for grouping their questions into four categories.

1. Best experience from the past.
2. What do we appreciate from what we have in the present?
3. Where do we want to go? (Dream Big)
4. How to get there? (Grouping ideas, assigning task forces, championing efforts, creating a Project Implementation Plan.)

As you can see, this formula is not very different from the constructive feedback formula. Because we mentioned that people are more likely to be sincere and share their experiences if we ask about their best experience, Appreciative Inquiry practitioners suggest taking inspiration from the best experience that had occurred in the past.

So, the formula in the nutshell is:

Best (in past+in present+in future) + how to get there in the best possible way.

These questions are drastically different from regular interview questions in journalism. The goal of these questions is to collect as many ideas as possible. The goal of the regular interview is to collect as many readers as possible. Readers like conflicts. Conflicts scare team members and they might feel that it is not safe to share their experiences.

As mentioned before, the point is not to avoid discussing conflict, but to provide the tools that will make the discussion more constructive.

Example

Research Question: How to create a secure environment in the classroom, so that everyone is encouraged to participate and contribute to the discussion?

1. Questions about a High Point in the Past
   a. Think of a time when you first learnt that your voice matters, and you could bring about a positive change. What was that experience like?
   b. How did it feel?
   c. What triggered your actions?
   d. Was there an essential need to contribute with your suggestion?
   e. Was there someone you were advocating for?
   f. What pushed you out of your comfort zone?

Lesson 14: The Magic Formula for Empowering Questions

    g. What made you feel secure to step up and speak up?
    h. How did that experience shape your future career path?

2. Questions about your strengths in the present
    a. In your current position, what gives you life professionally?
    b. What keeps you going?
    c. What is the best part about your job?
    d. What gives you professional satisfaction?
    e. What do you value about your job?

3. Questions to research the actual topic of interest
    a. How do you create the ideal learning environment for your trainees?
    b. What do you do to encourage participation?
    c. How do you motivate sincerity?
    d. How do you reward the idea of contributing to the group discussion?
    e. What else is important for creating an ideal learning environment?
        - How do you motivate that new item?
        - What gives life to that new item?
    f. What else is important for best serving the needs of the learning community?
        - How do you motivate that new item?
        - What gives life to that new item?

4. Questions about dreaming big
    a. In an ideal world, what kind of interactions do

you want to see between the trainers and trainees?
b. What are the features of ideal trainers?
c. What are the features of ideal trainees?

5. Questions about how to get to those big dreams
   a. What do you need to shape and maintain that best team?
   b. Have you thought about how to communicate those needs to the powers that be?

Exercise 14.1 — Practicing Appreciative Questioning

Pick one of the reframed topics you developed in Exercise 10.2. Identify the stakeholders interested in that topic. For example, in the case above, stakeholders could include students, teachers, parents, school administrators, etc.

Develop a set of questions using the following formula:

Best (in the past + in the present + in the future) + How to get there in the best possible way.

Ask your questions of the stakeholders identified and collect a set of answers. Write a conclusion.

In my class of displaced children from Artsakh, one of their biggest concerns was finding new friends. Children from the same village—many of them close friends, classmates, and neighbors—were now relocated to various parts of a new country. Many of them saw our online communication as a time to reconnect with their friends. However, we came up with an exercise where they could pick a new classmate and interview them to research what constitutes friendship. Many of them developed good relationships with their interviewees and reported receiving additional invitations for playdates. Some even requested adding their new friends to our online meetings.

Appendix A suggests some questions about ideal friendship.

Questions for Managing Up

Managing up is the process of developing a positive and effective relationship with your boss(es) to better align with their expectations and goals while ensuring your own productivity and job satisfaction. It helps mitigate misunderstandings and conflict, and helps you and your team to thrive. It also builds trust and suggests opportunities to grow.

Below are some suggested questions to help you to manage up.

1. Would it help you to know how to get the best possible out of me in this project?
2. Here's where I'm strongest and where you can count on me.
3. I'm still learning in these areas and could use a little extra patience or guidance.
4. I really enjoy these types of tasks and would love to help with them.
5. I would need more help or a clearer explanation with these tasks.
6. When I do well, this is how I feel most encouraged.
7. When I'm struggling, giving me time to figure it out helps me the most.

If you feel the timing is right, you might choose to interview your boss using these questions. I tested them on my own boss as part of a planned semi-annual performance evaluation. At the time, I was completing my Appreciative Inquiry Certification training with Champlain College's David Cooperrider Center for Appreciative Inquiry in Burlington, Vermont. My boss was so intrigued by these questions that she turned them around and asked me to answer them honestly and sincerely for her. This conversation significantly improved our relationship.

In addition, I started including the following quote in my email signature:

> "A leader's job is to make the strengths of people effective and their weaknesses irrelevant."
>
> — PETER DRUCKER

CONCLUSION

Over the course of these lessons, we have learned about various methods of communication. We have learned about the importance of assuming good intent, staying positive, and crafting powerful questions. We have learned about the importance of sincerity and the discussion of the most challenging items with a positive attitude.

I want to give you one more life example about the use of Appreciative Inquiry at the time of distress.

> While our classes with the pilot team of children from Artsakh continued, the ceasefire was broken several times during our first semester. After one of the shelling of a civilian vehicle, I noticed that the children were scared. Not knowing how to reframe, I asked: "Do you have a designated shelter, a place where you can wait comfortably during the next shelling?" The kids started texting in a panic that none of their villages had bomb shelters. Then someone typed that their school has a pretty deep and large basement and that was the only place for the villagers to hide during the shellings. Someone from

another village responded that their school basement is designated for that purpose too. In the following week, during our appreciation exercise, some of the kids reported that they contacted their village administration, got in touch with their school supply person, went house to house to collect mattresses and blankets, placed big pots in the basement, filled them up with drinking water, brought empty buckets to use as a toilet, and even brought their favorite Harry Potter volumes to start a bomb shelter library.

Appreciative Inquiry is the ability to see the problem, but also have the skill of recovering from the initial shock quickly, reframing the situation, and thinking more intensely in the direction of finding the solution. To get to that point, one might need to do daily exercises to practice mindfulness, to create new neurological connections in their brains, and to develop new patterns of thinking. Listing daily the things they appreciate in their lives and the things that they do with joy helps to create that pattern.

When discussing the importance of withholding the initial reaction, we appraised this ability that makes us, humans, different from the rest of the animal world. Humans learned to tame their instinct and withhold their initial reaction because it helped them to mitigate conflicts and survive. Understanding culpability helps prevent victim-blaming, while recognizing intent to harm allows us to distinguish between accidental harm and malicious intent. There are situations that we have little control over; however, once we distinguish between accidental and intentional, we can decide more quickly whether it is safer to act or to ask for additional help. This is why it is so crucial to separate actions that are not forbidden by the law from illegal actions, separate constitutional actions from unconstitutional, understand the difference in crimes that are simple versus those that are aggravated, and involuntary actions versus crimes involving moral turpitude.

Understanding these nuances allows us to be more self-confident in making the assumption of good intent. Assuming good intent helps us to shift paradigms and think beyond traditional limitations.

We discussed five principles of Appreciative Inquiry (3, 8–10):

1. Constructionist Principle
2. Poetic Principle
3. Simultaneity Principle
4. Anticipatory Principle
5. Positivity Principle

In some other textbooks you may find the following five phases of Appreciative Inquiry:

The 5-D Model of Appreciative Inquiry (3, 5–7):

1. Define: choose a positive, meaningful topic.
2. Discover: explore and appreciate what currently exists that works well.
3. Dream: envision a compelling future to spark creativity and excitement.
4. Design: plan and prioritise actions to achieve the dream.
5. Deliver: implement and sustain the change.

The 5-I Model of Appreciative Inquiry (8):

1. Initiate: Begin the process by identifying the focus of inquiry and engaging stakeholders.
2. Inquire: Explore and discover the organization's strengths and successes through appreciative interviews.
3. Imagine: Envision possibilities for the future by building on the strengths identified.
4. Innovate: Design and develop strategies to achieve the envisioned future.
5. Implement: Execute the strategies and monitor progress to ensure sustainable change.

In this book I have tried to intertwine these models and their five principles. In translation of this theory into Armenian, I have not aligned these concepts with a specific letter of the alphabet. My goal has been to convey the message with the words that work best. The main idea to remember is that by using Appreciative Inquiry you go through the same cycle of project implementation, choosing to work around a positive core.

The goal is to stay positive and creative, to be bold but respectful, to improvise, to concentrate on what you want more of, to dream big, to be delicate and diplomatic, to be assertive, genuinely inquisitive and industrious.

To conclude, I want to leave you with a Native American parable about two wolves (9).

The Parable of Two Wolves

One evening, an elder sat with his grandson by the fire. After a moment of silence, the elder said,

> "A fight is going on inside me. It's a terrible fight between two wolves.
>
> One wolf is evil—he is anger, envy, greed, arrogance, resentment, lies, and selfishness.
>
> The other wolf is good—he is joy, peace, love, hope, humility, kindness, empathy, and truth.
>
> This same fight is happening inside you—and inside every other person, too."
>
> The grandson thought about it for a while, then asked, "Grandfather, which wolf will win?"
>
> The elder smiled and replied,
>
> "The one you feed."

APPENDIX A: SELECTED EXERCISE ANSWERS

These answers serve as a guide and may vary based on individual interpretation.

Exercise 2.1

1. Accuser: "You always ruin my plans."
   Affirmative: "I've noticed that our programs sometimes don't develop as expected, and that's been difficult for me. How can we work together to improve them?"

2. An insult. "You are one of the lazy ones, you never help me with the housework."
   Affirmative: "I've been overwhelmed with housework lately. Can we discuss how to share the responsibilities more evenly?"

3. Accuser: "You're always late, and that's disrespectful."
   Affirmative: "Starting on time is extremely important to me.

Appendix A: Selected Exercise Answers

Delays make me extremely stressed. Can we work out a solution together?"

4. Threatening: "You're such a slacker in the group project!"
Assertive: "I've observed that our contributions to the project might be uneven. How about we brainstorm ways to ensure everyone's pulling their weight?"

5. Accusatory: "You never appreciate what I do for you!"
Assertive: "I've been feeling like my efforts might not be fully appreciated. Can we talk about ways to acknowledge each other more?"

6. Threatening: "You make everything about yourself!"
Assertive: "I've noticed that our conversations sometimes focus more on one person. Can we work on making them more balanced?"

7. Accusatory: "You're always interrupting me!"
Assertive: "I've felt interrupted during our discussions. How can we make sure both of us have a chance to express our thoughts?"

8. Threatening: "You're such a gossip; you talk behind everyone's back!"
Assertive: "I've heard some conversations that feel like gossip. Can we find ways to promote positive communication?"

9. Accusatory: "You never support me in my decisions!"
Assertive: "I've sensed a lack of support in some of my decisions. How can we ensure we're on the same page and supportive of each other?"

Appendix A: Selected Exercise Answers

Exercise 8.1

Negative: Reducing Energy Waste
Positive: Optimizing Energy Efficiency

Negative: Eliminating Customer Complaints
Positive: Enhancing Customer Satisfaction

Negative: Preventing System Downtime
Positive: Ensuring System Reliability and Uptime

Negative: Decreasing Unemployment Rates
Positive: Increasing Employment Opportunities

Negative: Limiting Traffic Accidents
Positive: Improving Road Safety

Negative: Addressing Poor Academic Performance
Positive: Boosting Academic Excellence

Negative: Reducing Food Waste
Positive: Promoting Food Conservation and Resourcefulness

Negative: Avoiding Financial Losses
Positive: Securing Financial Growth

Negative: Stopping Cybersecurity Breaches
Positive: Strengthening Digital Security

Negative: Reducing Water Shortages
Positive: Ensuring Sustainable Water Management

Appendix A: Selected Exercise Answers

Exercise 10.2

Step Two: Improving public transportation to serve commuters better.
Step Three: Gaining insights from commuters on how to design a more effective and enjoyable transportation system.

Step Two: Encouraging teenagers to participate in civic activities.
Step Three: Empowering teenagers to lead community initiatives and shape a more dynamic civic culture.

Step Two: Helping local communities adapt to environmental challenges.
Step Three: Learning innovative, eco-friendly practices from local communities to enhance sustainability efforts globally.

Exercise 14.1

1. Think of your best friend. What is the best memory that you have of that person?

2. Why do you consider that person your best friend? What are the qualities that you like about that person the most?

3. How many good, reliable friends do you have? Why do you consider them to be good and reliable?

4. What is the ideal friendship for you? What kind of relationship with your friends do you want to have in an ideal world?

5. How do you plan to strengthen your relationship with your friends? How do you see yourself getting from what you have now to what is ideal for you?

APPENDIX B: BIBLIOGRAPHY

1. Jacqueline Kelm. *The Joy of Appreciative Living*, Penguin Book, 2008. ISBN-978-1-58542-660-7

2. Robyn Stratton-Berkessel. *Appreciative Inquiry for Collaborative Solutions: 21 Strength-Based Workshops*, John Whiley and Sons, Inc., 2010. ISBN-10: 0470483164.

3. David L. Cooperrider, Diana Whitney, and Jacqueline M. Stavros. *Appreciative Inquiry Handbook For Leaders of Change*, Second Edition, Crown Customs Publishing, Inc. and Berrett-Koehler Publishers, Inc., 2008. ISBN-978-1-57675-493-1.

4. Fran Peavey. "Strategic Questioning Manual," *The Commons Social Change Library* Commonslibrary.org, 2019. Available at https://commonslibrary.org/wp-content/uploads/strat_questioning_manual.pdf. Accessed February 4, 2025.

5. Hovhannes Tumanyan. *Մի կաթիլ մեղրը* [A Drop of Honey], *Grqaser*, n.d. Retrieved from https://www.grqaser.org/en/books/75 (in Armenian). Accessed February 4, 2025.

6. Atabek Khnkoyan. *Մկների ժողովը* [The Meeting of Mice]. *Poqrik.am*, n.d. Retrieved from https://poqrik.am/մանկական-գրադարան/խնկո-ապեր-աթաբեկ-խնկոյան-բանաստեղծու/ (In Armenian). Accessed February 4, 2025.

7. Finckenauer, *Legal Socialization: Concepts and Practices*, 1998; Trinkner & Cohn, 2014.

8. David L. Cooperrider and Diana Whitney. *Appreciative Inquiry: A Positive Revolution in Change*. Berrett-Koehler Publishers, 2005.

9. Author Unknown. "*Two Wolves—A Cherokee Parable*", *Sapphyr.net*, (n.d.)

Appendix B: Bibliography

Retrieved from https://www.sapphyr.net/natam/two-wolves.htm. Accessed February 4, 2025.

10. Diana Whitney, Amanda Trosten-Bloom, David Cooperrider, and Brian Kaplan. *Encyclopedia of Positive Questions*. ISBN-10: 1933403128.

11. Jane Watkins, Bernard Mohr, and Ralph Kelly. *Appreciative Inquiry: Change at the Speed of Imagination*, John Whiley and Sons, Inc., 2011. ISBN-10: 0470527978.

12. *Odyssey of the Mind*, https://odysseyofthemind.com/, Accessed February 4, 2025.

ABOUT THE AUTHOR

Arpi Arus (pen name) is a Vermont-based scholar with 35 years of project management experience in international humanitarian organizations. She has worked in several conflict zones across the Caucasus and former Yugoslavia and has been a visiting scholar at the Economics Institute in Boulder, Colorado, and the Massachusetts Institute of Technology. She holds a Master's degree in Intercultural Service, Leadership, and Management from the School for International Training, Brattleboro, VT. Her passion for community development has shaped her career, and by integrating Appreciative Inquiry with Intercultural Communication, she aims to enhance the quality and impact of development projects. Her most recent work with children from Artsakh (also known as Nagorno-Karabakh) was so impactful that she created this guide to help train more facilitators. The goal is to support the organic, community-driven integration of forcefully displaced populations with native communities in conflict-affected areas.

ABOUT THE ARTIST

Milena Avetisyan was eight years old when four new children from war-affected areas joined her class. Her elementary school struggled to accommodate the influx of displaced families with young children. During that time, Milena's artwork was so vivid and inspiring that it caught the attention of her local teacher and the Armenian community in Vermont. Moved by her talent, they compiled her artwork into a calendar to raise funds for forcibly displaced families. The cover image of this book, in particular, inspired the author to start an online class on Appreciative Inquiry for those affected by the war.

www.ingramcontent.com/pod-product-compliance
Lightning Source LLC
Chambersburg PA
CBHW020551030426
42337CB00013B/1047